PERFECT PETS

by Jill McDougall

OXFORD
UNIVERSITY PRESS
AUSTRALIA & NEW ZEALAND

OXFORD
UNIVERSITY PRESS

Oxford University Press is a department of the University of Oxford.
It furthers the University's objective of excellence in research,
scholarship, and education by publishing worldwide. Oxford is a
registered trademark of Oxford University Press in the UK and in
certain other countries.

Published in Australia by
Oxford University Press
Level 8, 737 Bourke Street, Docklands, Victoria 3008, Australia

ISBN 9780190316778

Illustrations by Helen Dardik
Designed by Oxford University Press in collaboration with Ana Cosma
Printed in China by Leo Paper Products Ltd

Acknowledgements

Series Editor: Nikki Gamble

The publishers would like to thank the following for the permission to
reproduce photographs:

p1: Ace Stock Limited/Alamy; **p4/5**: Emery Way/Getty Images;
p5t: Ron Levine/Getty Images;
p6/7: Vita Khorzhevska/Shutterstock; **p7t**: Odilon Dimier/PhotoAlto/
Getty Images; **p8/9**: Michiel de Wit/Shutterstock; **p9t**: Ace Stock Limited/
Alamy; **p10/11**: Zadiraka Evgenii/Shutterstock; **p11t**: Noel Hendrickson/
Masterfile; **p12/13**: Anthony Lee/Getty Images; **p13t**: Stephen Simpson/
Getty Images; **p14/15**: Michael Jung/Shutterstock; **p14t**: Emery Way/
Getty Images; **p15br**: Nattika/Shutterstock; **p15tl**: Vita Khorzhevska/
Shutterstock; **p15ml**: Michiel de Wit/Shutterstock; **p15tr**: Zadiraka
Evgenii/Shutterstock; **p15mr**: Anthony Lee/Getty Images

Cover photograph: Marija Savic/Stocksy

Contents

This book will help you pick your perfect pet!

Super Dogs

Dogs are great pets because they like to play.

But did you know that dogs have *super* powers?

Dogs can hear sounds that we can't hear. They are super sniffers, too. Dogs can smell at least 1000 times better than people can.

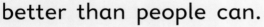

Meet my pet

Amy's dog is called Jazz.
Jazz likes to go to the park with Amy.

Is a dog your perfect pet?

Pros

- clever
- loyal

Cons

- leaves poo to be picked up
- can be noisy

Cuddly Cats

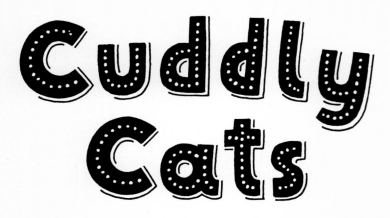

Cats make cuddly pets and
they talk to you, too!
A "meow" can mean
"play with me" or "pat me".
A loud meow could mean
"Feed me!". (Cats can be bossy!)

Cats are sleepy pets. They sleep
for about 15 hours every day.

Meow!

Meet my pet

Luke's cat is called Pixie.
Pixie likes to chase toys.

Is a cat your perfect pet?

Pros
♥ playful
♥ clean

Cons
♠ **sheds** fur
♠ has sharp claws

Clever Geckos

If you don't have much space,
a gecko could be your perfect pet.

Geckos are little lizards.
Most are good climbers.
Their feet stick to walls
to help them climb. They can
even walk upside down!

Meet my pet

Molly's gecko is called Tinsel.
Tinsel likes to climb – onto Molly's head!

Is a gecko your perfect pet?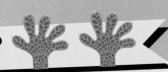

Pros
- ♥ easy to look after
- ♥ quiet

Cons
- ♠ can be shy
- ♠ needs to eat living **prey**

Skinny Stick Insects

Stick insects look amazing!
They are long and thin,
just like sticks. Stick insects
are the longest insects.

A stick insect's leg can fall off ...
but sometimes it can grow a
new one!

Meet my pet

Tim's stick insect is called Twiggy. Twiggy likes to walk on Tim's hand.

Is a stick insect your perfect pet?

Pros

♥ quiet

♥ clean

Cons

♠ has lots of babies (if it's a female!)

♠ can't really play with you

Busy Chickens

Would you like a pet that lives outside? If so, a chicken might be your perfect pet!

Chickens like to be busy. They scratch in the dirt, looking for bugs to eat. Chickens like to have a bath ... in the dust! This is how they look after their feathers.

Meet my pet

Jake's chicken is called Lola. Lola likes to follow Jake around.

Is a chicken your perfect pet?

Pros
♥ fun to feed
♥ lays eggs

Cons
♥ noisy
♥ needs space outside

Pick Your Perfect Pet

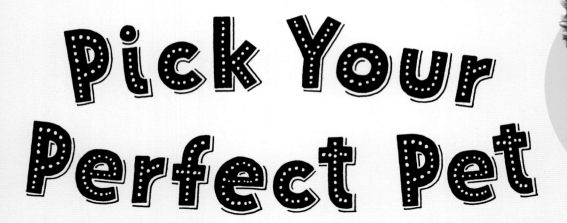

1. Talk to your family to find out what they think about getting a pet.

2. Find out more about some different pets. You could even look after one for a day.

3. Look at the pros and cons of the pets. Then score each pet with your family.

4. Decide which pet is perfect for you.

Meet my pet

Which is your perfect pet?

Pet	Score (out of 5)
dog	🐾🐾
cat	🥣🥣🥣🥣🥣
gecko	🐾🐾🐾🐾
stick insect	— —
chicken	🥚

15

Glossary

loyal: will always be there for you

prey: an animal that is eaten by another animal

sheds: takes off or drops a covering, such as fur or skin

Index